Published by Geddes & Grosset,
David Dale House, New Lanark, ML11 9DJ, Scotland

© 1996 Geddes & Grosset

First published 1996
Reprinted 2001

ISBN  1 85534 169 7

Printed and bound in China

# The Snowman

Judy Hamilton
Illustrated by Mark Ripley

## Tarantula Books

Brand-new and sparkling white, the snowman did not know much at all about the world. The afternoon he was made, he caught sight of the setting sun glowing red in the sky.

"He looks fierce," thought the snowman, "but I'm sure he can't hurt me." He watched it go down and disappear.

Evening fell and the moon rose in the sky—a full moon, round and white. The snowman thought it was the sun again.

"He's back!" the snowman said. "Oh dear! Well, never mind. At least I can see now."

"I can see," said the snowman to himself, "but I can't move. I do wish I could run in the snow and slide on the ice like the children do!"

The old watchdog, chained to his kennel nearby, heard the snowman.

"The sun will soon teach you to run, just like the snowmen before you—ARF! ARF!" the dog laughed hoarsely. "Up there in the sky is the moon. He can't do anything. But remember that red thing in the sky before that? That was the sun. He'll be back tomorrow and *he'll* get you moving—ARF! ARF!"

"I don't know if I like the sound of that," said the snowman.

"Too bad—ARF! ARF!" chuckled the watchdog. He huddled up in the corner of his kennel and went to sleep.

The snowman, of course, stayed up all night. He saw the grey mist of dawn and felt the frost set a sparkle on his stony smile and give a crunch to his carroty nose. He saw the sun rise and set the snow-laden branches of the trees a-shimmer.

It was bitterly cold and beautiful—perhaps the sun wasn't so bad?

"What a wonderfully beautiful day! I do so love winter days like this!"

A young girl, hand-in-hand with her boyfriend, had come into the garden. The girl's face was alight with pleasure at the snow. "Isn't he a fine fellow!" she said to her boyfriend. The young man laughed and pulled her by the hand back towards the house.

The snowman's heart swelled with pride at the girl's words.

"Who are they?" he asked the watchdog. "Do you know?"

"ARF! ARF! I know everything and everyone!" barked the watchdog. "Those two are a pair; they're mates. They like each other more than anything else. But they like me too; they give me bones!" he said proudly.

"Are they important, like you and me?" asked the snowman.

"Don't you know anything?" said the old dog. "Why do you think we are outside in the cold while they have a nice warm kennel over there?" He pointed to the farmhouse with his grey-haired old nose. "Of course they are important! It is we who are not!"

"But I like the cold!" protested the snowman.

The dog wasn't listening. He was gazing towards the farmhouse.

"I was important once," he rasped. "ARF! ARF! Oh yes, they all loved me when I was a pup. I sat on their laps and licked their faces, and the master told me how clever I was. When I grew too big to sit on laps, they gave me my own bed in the kitchen—a nice soft cushion beside the stove. Plenty of food there was—good food too!—and peace and quiet. And how I loved that stove!"

"What's a stove?" said the snowman.

"I was forgetting," said the dog, "that you know nothing. A stove is a wonderful thing. It is coal black, just like your eyes, and it has four legs, just as I have. People feed it coal and logs, and it shoots flames from its mouth. When the wind blows hard enough, it roars and makes a howling sound with its long black neck. To lie beside a stove is one of the nicest things to do in all the world. ARF! ARF!"

The old dog's eyes grew misty with the memory.

"What does it look like?" asked the snowman.

The dog's grey muzzle pointed to a window in the farmhouse. The snowman looked and saw the black thing, gleaming with polish, flames dancing behind its glass door. He could not stop looking.

He had never seen such a beautiful thing. He felt drawn towards it.

Why should this be? A snowman needs the cold to live. Why should he want to be close to a stove?

"Oh, why did you leave her," he said to the dog, "when she is so lovely?"

"I bit the master's boy and they threw me out," complained the dog.

The snowman stared at the stove. "Such elegant legs!" he thought. "Such a beautiful face!"

"I feel so strange!" he said to the dog. "My insides are crumbling. I would dearly love to go inside beside the stove. If I wish very hard, do you think that it might happen? It is my only wish in the whole world."

"ARF! ARF! Not a chance of it!" laughed the dog. "And if you did get inside, it would be the end of you!"

"This feeling may be the end of me," moaned the snowman, "for it is cracking me up."

All day long, the snowman gazed mournfully at the stove. He watched them open it to feed it with logs and gasped with delight when he saw the flames and sparks shooting out from its red mouth. As the afternoon wore on and it grew dark in the kitchen, the snowman marvelled at the hot red glow that he could still see through the gloom from his position in the garden.

The old watchdog grumbled in puzzlement. Why did the snowman feel this way?

All night long, the snowman stood dreaming in the garden while the frost got busy about him, decorating the trees with dainty ice crystals, creeping into the bones of the old watchdog and making him growl.

Next morning was colder than ever. Ice covered the windows of the farmhouse and blocked out the snowman's view of the stove. He pined all day. The dog growled in disgust.

"Such foolishness!" he said. "But my bones tell me the weather will change soon. That'll be the end of it all!"

Sure enough, next day it was warmer. It began to thaw. The snowman began to melt. First his carroty nose fell out, then his teeth and eyes. His head was falling to bits, and his body was sinking.

One morning the dog woke to see that all that remained of the snowman was a heap of wet snow. In the middle of the heap lay a great long poker, used to pin the snowman's head to his body.

"That's the poker for the stove!" said the dog. "No wonder he felt as if he belonged beside her! But that's the end of it! Spring's coming, it'll all be forgotten!"

And the old dog was right.